The Soul of Sarah

Five Lessons For My Daughters

Christian B. Winters

Morgan Anne Winters

The Soul of Sarah

Copyright © 2024 Christian Bernard Winters
All rights reserved.
ISBN: 9798325596483

Foreword

Sarai! Welcome to the day that will change your life forever!

"Sarai?" you may ask, "You don't even know my name." Oh, but I do. The Bible says Sarai was barren, and she had no child. The fact that you and I are speaking now tells me that something deep inside you or the person who gave you this book recognizes that there lies something miraculous, yet dormant, in your spirit that must come alive!

So, get as excited for yourself as I am for you because the moment you decide to start and finish reading The Soul of Sarah, one of two, if not both, of these things, will happen to you:

>   1. You will be inspired and equipped to go and find the Sarah you need to birth

yourself into your next dimension of greatness
2. You will become the Sarah you need to birth those waiting for you into their next dimension of greatness.

Either way, the essence of the woman will emerge. What is that essence? Well, my favorite way to articulate the nature of a woman is to explain that she is a woman. Woman – a man with a womb. As it is in the natural, so is it in the Spirit, so you, woman, are blessed with all of the God-gifted attributes of a man. Moreover, you are incredibly gifted with an ability that man does not possess the unique ability to take a seed, incubate it, and make it far more than what it was when it was given to you. Because of your womb, you take in seed and give back babies; you take in a word and make it a book; you take in a house and transform it into a home. You are extraordinary!

And still, as remarkable as you are, there are barren places that your God wants revived in you, so do not laugh, Sarai. Believe. You are holding the right book. I gladly receive the honor of recommending the work of Christian Winters to you. It is inspired by a woman too great for me even to describe my time here. It is inspired by a lady who was to us and to every single life she ever touched, and know that she touched hundreds of thousands with her effortless, passionate service and love.

She is our Sarah. She is Sondra Elizabeth Winters, our late mother.

Through her seed of life, Christian, the Bearer of Christ, Sarai is ushered into a time and space where you will be renamed Sarah. Christian Winters will teach you incredible, practical, biblical lessons from the life of this heroine, Sarah. You'll read about how to manage your emotions, escape living a haphazard lifestyle, and gain unwavering belief in yourself! You will be moved by his encouragement and explanations of becoming agreeable instead of argumentative. Most of all, you will enter into an understanding of how God will change your name, your mind, and your reality so that what was once barren becomes an oasis of abundance from which you live your wildest dreams!

Sound Interesting? Then, quickly turn the page and enter into the Soul of Sarah.

Jéneen Winters-Barlow

Lessons

Introduction 9
Lesson ONE: 21
Lesson TWO: The Will, Seeding You Ability 33
Lesson THREE: The Emotions, Expanding Your Ability 41
Lesson FOUR: Beholding Your Ability 53
   A Daughter's Response, Morgan Winters: ... 56
Lesson Five: How To Know Identify Who To Say I Do To? 65

The Soul of Sarah

Introduction

On the morning of January 28, 2011, with great gaze and courage, my sister poured her last sentiments on our mother through liturgical dance. The crowd watched closely as each and every move told of the years our mother covered us with indescribable care, love, and counsel. I believe she gave everything to us, withholding nothing. Jeneen danced to a song called, Alabaster Box by CeCe Winans. The song describes what it means to adorn someone whose goodness is impossible to repay. The religious of this world turn their noses at the thought of pouring all of your honor upon another human being. But when you realize that God gifted you that person, you'll fully understand how due that person is to your honor. On the day of our mother's final goodbye, my sister worshipped

God as I had never seen; she danced until she had nothing left to honor our Sarah, Sondra Elizabeth Winters.

My sister's ministry ultimately empowered me to go forward in mine that morning. I approached the podium, trembling at the thought that I was eulogizing my last parent. I had just eulogized my father five years before. For many years, I've heard, read, and even taught people how to use the life of the Biblical hero, Sarah. I observed her commitment, decisions, sacrifices, and great and not-so-great days. I was unsure of what the last words over my mother should be. I had just turned thirty-two years of age. I had suffered more than I could ever understand, and all I could do was ask the most common question people ask when someone dies, "What happened?" The physical cause of Mom's death was pancreatic cancer, but I was convinced that her sickness didn't fully answer that question. She was too vast, not only because she was my mother but simply because she was a woman. I forced myself wholeheartedly into the question because I needed an answer. I was a depleted leader and a dismantled son. I gazed into my mother's character, hidden achievements, and passive, assertive demeanor until I knew exactly what happened.

*"When Sarah was 127 years old, **she died** at Kiriath-Arba (now called Hebron) in the land of Canaan. There, Abraham mourned and wept for her. Then, leaving her body, he said to the Hittite elders, "Here I am, a stranger and a foreigner among you. Please sell me a piece of land so I can give my wife a **proper burial**."*

Genesis 23:1-4 NLT

Sarah died, that's what happened. There was no better way to eulogize my mother. I now had more than an answer to the question, I found a revelation inside of tragedy. I shared a message called the *"The Soul of Sarah."* I felt compelled to help women rediscovery their Capacity. There was no better way to honor our mother my than to lift up woman. A woman can take the seed of a man which measures in size of 1000th of a millimeter and with time give the world a human being. She then takes that tiny human and nurtures it into an adult with their own things to birth. The thought arrested my mind, then opened my soul to a weighty thought. I considered about the grief that families, suppressive cultures, organizations and governments will to continue to suffer by a refusal to engage the strategic mastery that every woman is born with.

    I felt the unction to teach women the depth of Sarah's soul in a world where only the seed of Abraham is discussed. His seed had to be accepted, developed, and birthed by a God-gifted woman for the world to see Abraham's many nations. Every woman is born with the same grace. Every woman has something specific that the world needs. The Soul of Sarah is not something you gain by a simple prayer. The success of this journey is steeped in your commitment to develop and maintain the health of your God-given, *spiritual reproduction system*, which I explain in this book. You are reading this book today because a remarkably creative, extremely determined woman is in you. God put her there; it is well past time to discover, empower, and activate all of her. You are more than just some woman who will pass through this life and die. You are more than someone's wife, lover, mother, businesswoman, or congregant serving faithfully in a congregation. You are a woman able to usher greatness into the world around you.

God created the world and a man to take dominion over it. This man, Adam, was given an extraordinary amount of authority. He was empowered to assign an identity to everything God created simply by naming it. It gets even deeper! All things were subject to this man's authority. He named all that was created, tended to it, and ensured it stayed the course of its original intent. ***As incredible as all of that was, Adam was missing something! He named plenty but created nothing.*** I believe that when God said, "It is not good for man to be alone," He was not giving man someone to go on a date. God was providing for man the one thing he would never have otherwise: the ability to create. This alone makes women unique. This is the foundation upon which the thoughts in this book are written.

A woman's reproductive system includes four major parts:

1. The ovaries produce the egg that receives seed from a man who adores her;
2. The fallopian tubes are the tunnel the ova travels through toward the womb. This is also where conception takes place.
3. The womb serves as the home to the developing fetus
4. Finally, the birth canal releases her creation into the hands of the one who gave her the seed from the beginning.

My sister and I were not there to watch our births, but we were blessed to watch how our mother continually birthed us throughout our lives. Her love and mothering adorned us until the day the Lord took her. Mothers don't just birth a child and walk away. A woman uses the same intensity of getting her children through the world as it took to get them into the world. She is committed to pushing them into the next dream, the next hope, and the next reality.

God made the male species masterfully, but the best that man can do in terms of creating a child is to lend a woman a seed. The male sperm is so small that it cannot even be measured in millimeters. Scientists had to create another scale of measurement called a micrometer to estimate the size of a sperm, so a micrometer is equivalent to 1000th of a millimeter. It is staggering to fathom how a woman can receive something finite and, with time, nurture, and nature, produce a person with five senses, working organs, and a brain that allows that created person to function in this world. Simply amazing!

Even more masterful is that a woman can take any seed through the same process. She can give life to anything that she decides to internalize. No matter how small, she has the innate ability to make great. She does it through a God-given spiritual reproductive system that mimics the natural reproductive system. The same way her ovaries, fallopian tubes, womb, and birth canal operate to form and birth a child is the same way her mind, will, emotions, and declaration operate to create any greatness she wants to see in the world. Each part functions in a different capacity, but together, they bring beauty to what was just a seed at first. Once a woman becomes aware of this innate gift, she will become more cautious about what she allows. The spiritual reproductive system doesn't just work when it receives a positive seed. It can also shape something negative.

This is vital information for our daughters as they develop into the emotionally tumultuous world of womanhood. This knowledge becomes the guiding light for everyday decisions. Throughout history and even now, women are seen as second class to men. Religious institutions have ushered sexism into society by teaching concepts like "the weaker vessel" and "submission" out of context to subdue the strength of women. Let us dispel the misunderstanding of the weaker vessel. By nature, she is not built like a man. The weaker vessel has all to do with a woman's physical makeup, not her inability to achieve certain feats. Her stature is only a reminder of what she was created to do and be. She was not made to push and pull her way through life. She was created to bring shape to what she receives by grace.

These concepts were never introduced for women's captivity but rather for their protection because of her value. There are only two reasons God commands her to be submitted. Firstly, He knows that what he made is too powerful to be left vulnerable. The second is that the one to whom she is submitted will protect the sanctity of the only gateway into the human world: women!

The Soul of Sarah

Lesson ONE:

The Mind, Releasing Your Ability

Genesis 17:15, 16 "God also said to Abraham, 'As for Sarai, your wife, you are no longer to call her Sarai; her name will be Sarah. I will bless her and will surely give you a son by her. I will bless her so that she will be the mother of nations; kings of peoples will come from her."

Sarah needed to know that her mind was her servant, not her master. You are the master of what you allow your mind to be opened to. God made a great Man, a great promise. The description of this promise was amazingly vast. He would be the producer of a great nation. His lineage was described to be as immeasurable as the stars of the sky or the sand of the ground. This great promise would happen despite his ninety-nine years on the earth. Then, the Lord told him that his name must be changed so that his persona would match his promise. Abram's name was changed to Abraham because he was to become the father of many nations.

"Wherever there is a father and a promise on a great nation,
there must be a mother equipped to bring forth such greatness."

As soon as the Lord finished speaking to Abram about the greatness coming from him, He began to talk about the gateway that all of this greatness had to pass through. It was impossible to get this promise of God in the world other than through Sarah. God first told Abram to call her by a different name, just as God did his. It was pertinent that since God changed Abraham's name, he would call his wife by a different name. Calling her by a new name would change her thinking about herself. This mind change would prepare her entire body for the future that was before her. Even though she was ninety and past the childbearing age, the resurrected mind forced the ability left in her body to rise. Just as the natural reproductive system's ovaries release eggs that will be seeded, so does the mind operate. The mind of a Sarah is not closed to divine opportunity. In other words, she is not closed-minded. She allows herself to think vastly because a vast God created her. It is natural for a woman to approach situations cautiously because she is naturally graceful. Yet she is bold when her renewed mind quickens her greatness.

Her name was Sarai until Abraham was commanded to call her Sarah. The name Sarai means argumentative, while Sarah means agreeable. This is not to say that Sarai was argumentative in speech. We could never know that. Abraham is not here for us to ask. Let's clarify her position and why her name took on such meaning. We know that she was barren. Her barrenness led her into a conversation with God. She hid behind the doorway and laughed when told she would have a child. She also said, "Shall I have pleasure, my Lord, being that I am old." This is a revelation of what she had already determined about herself. She had reason to believe that she would never prosper in certain ways. God was aware of this, so he changed her name, which changed her mind and body. God is well aware of the things in your life that have caused you to determine that you will not succeed.. God makes promises that are in total disagreement with the negative things that cloud how you perceive yourself. He does this to give you a reason to change your mind. If God will get anything extraordinary done in your life, He has to challenge that argumentative nature until you are shaped to have an agreeable flow. The broken, disappointed parts of you argue over His will for you. This is not a place to be stuck. The barren areas of your life only follow the example of your closed mind.

"Call her Sarah!" God demanded Abraham. By this, she will know that a change has come. Every part of her will begin to agree with my promise, and her body will respond to the seed I have given you. A bound mind will not release spiritual Ova. I am sure there have been times when opportunity passed you by because your mind would not release anything you would receive. Sarai, you have missed relationships, career opportunities, and prophetic utterances because your current situation would not let your mind agree. Your mind is your servant. This means it cannot comfortably move without something telling it how to perform. The mind is eager to act, always searching for instruction. If this instruction does not flow from a healed you, it will act on the commands and issues of Sarai, which fight the call of greatness in your life. The changing of Sarah's name was not a play on words. Sarah was the mother of nations. Every time someone called Sarah or introduced herself to someone, she made a statement of faith. She was to call herself the mother of many nations even before she had a child. Sarah was a compassionate woman, and though she had become agreeable with the will of God, she allowed her emotions to shift her mental focus. Having no child yet and erroneously thinking it was her fault, she asked Abraham to have a child with their servant, Hagar. This was a mental error.

    The uncontrolled mind will not let you release yourself to awaiting greatness. Our conditions do not bind God, but we sometimes hinder him because of the argumentative nature of our minds. When you find yourself stuck between the bound nature of Sarai and Sarah's free life, it is not the time to decide life. Your decisions during these phases of life will only help further wound your emotions. These wounds will never remind you of what you are not capable of. The result of this constant reminder is that you'll find yourself in the destructive trap of comparison. This is where Sarah found herself. She invites a woman named Hagar, a servant girl, into her and her husband's bed to produce what she thought she couldn't. She forfeited her rights and gave her promise to another because she could not expand her mind. Do not sell yourself short by trying to achieve God's promises with a carnal mind. Feelings will come to challenge you, not to release your abilities. Know that they are only feelings. Your mind is God's gate. Keep it open.

Genesis 18:15 Sarah was afraid and denied it, saying, "I didn't laugh." But the LORD said, "No, you did laugh."

When you become a Sarah, you are guaranteed a conflict. This is not a sign that you are unworthy. It's a sign that the battle has begun. That's wonderful. Where there is no war, there is no change. Where there is no resistance, no strength is gained. The Lord asked her why she laughed, and she denied it. The religious teacher might argue that her laughter was a signal of weak faith. I would beg to differ. A great battle arises when you're about to become great. I would consider that her laughter resulted from the astonishment she experienced when she heard that something extraordinary was coming at a specific time. Her laughter was not disrespect to the declaration of God. It was the hard ground of her insecurities being jackhammered by the strong word of her God. It shook up everything she thought about herself, and it tickled her that she would experience life in the face of death. Her mind released the egg that would produce a nation. So, is it in the natural world? It is a particular time when a woman's body releases the egg, usually midway in the menstrual cycle; it is pushed down through the fallopian tubes and waits for the seed of the one who loves her.

Sometimes, it seems so hard to change your mind, and most times, it is because you believe that all that is involved in changing your mind is changing how you feel. It is impossible to base permanent decisions on feelings because of the pace at which they change. There are four significant factors that the truly changed mind rests on. We will discuss these further throughout this book.

Your Identity:

You will act like who you think you are. You will never do anything different than what you've convinced yourself you are. When you change your identity based on the definition God has established for you, you have gotten on the runway of life. Take Off.

Your Decision Making:

The new decisions you make as you develop through life cannot be made based on how you felt about your past but on what you learned from your past. When you master this, you will begin to decide based on who you've decided to become instead of who you were before.

Your Friendship Circle:

You need people around you who consistently affirm your change. These people always look at, talk about, and search for things beyond normal comprehension. Your friends are a portrait of who you will ultimately become. When Mary, the mother of Jesus, and Elizabeth, the mother of John, met, the fruit of their wombs leaped because they both possessed greatness.

Your Current Focus:

When you are driving a car, you will automatically begin to drift in the direction that you are looking. Your body begins to respond to your focus. You always move in the direction of your most dominant thought.

The Soul of Sarah

Lesson TWO:

The Will, Seeding You Ability

Genesis 21:1 "Now the LORD was gracious to Sarah as he had said, and the LORD did for Sarah what he had promised.

Sarah's will is her stubborn determination to make things happen. After she has released herself from her ill thinking toward herself and her future, Sarah is convinced that she can do it and will also do it. She realized that the act of change was more than a mere emotion. True change is an excavation. It is not only the digging up but the digging out of her past life that was important. Change removes the thoughts and negative self-perceptions that once locked her mind, thus locking her body. She had to change her decision-making. She could not continue to make decisions for her future based on old emotions. You cannot make changes simply based on how something made you feel before. You make changes based on what you've learned from how you felt. Sarah didn't open her mind and release her ability to receive God's promise because she felt bad about being barren. She opened her mind and released her ability because she learned who she was and discovered the untapped potential in a system that only seemed barren. Once she achieved this place, it was the beginning of her creativity. Her new decisions became aids to her future. As you become a Sarah, every decision daily is important to point toward your freshest desires.

You will always move in the direction of your most dominant thought. This is the beginning of your will. You have not done all this work to release your ability and then reject the seed of your future. Every Sarah has a stubborn determination. Like the fallopian tubes of the natural reproductive systems carry the released ova toward the womb, so does your will. It is said that this is where conception happens. It is tough to see a better day from where you are. Sometimes, you have to leave familiar thoughts and systems of belief to make healthy and fruitful connections. The philosophy behind moving forward is much simpler than how we treat it. You cannot sit and be constantly reminded of what you lack and believe you'll somehow gain more. It is better to move fearfully into the unknown than to die in the now that you know will eventually kill you. Sarah is never stagnant. She has a plan and places that she is stubbornly determined to go. This reminds me of the biblical story of the ten leprous men that Jesus healed.

And they lifted up [their] voices, and said, Jesus, Master, have mercy on us. And when he saw [them], he said unto them, Go show yourselves unto the priests. And it came to pass that, as they went, they were cleansed.

Luke 17:14:

    Once your abilities are released, you must continue forward until you have the power to conceive. This miracle with the leprous men was much different in how it was performed than usual. Most times, you find Jesus more hands-on in the miraculous. Here, you have men voicing their issues from afar. He doesn't lay his hands on them. He has no long dialogue. He doesn't refer to any laws or any prophets in a sermon to them. Jesus responds to their cry with a command from that same distance. He responds to their cry with a decree, "Go and show yourselves to the priest!" His words ignited their ability instead of encouraging their pity. Once they released their ability, they were commanded to move toward a place of proof. This is where conception happens. This is the commencement of the greatness that you will create. It is not until after you decide that you can create greatness that you will create greatness. This is where you really discover the power of your will. The will carries out the intentions of your heart. That is why it is important to express your desires; your will will stubbornly accomplish them. You will be challenged on this road. Remembering her former state, Sarah will question two major areas of her life.

1. She will question her worthiness.
2. She will also question her ability to complete the process.

When you have moved from stagnant to productive, these are natural questions, but they are not reasons to return to a barren belief system. You have to think through these questions with faith for your future and not the fear of your past. Women constantly battle with feeling worthy. Here is the answer. God created you worthy! He took time and created a divine system that continues to create within you. Events happen in life that test your thinking in this area. Perhaps you've used that system to birth things that weren't great. You have to move forward knowing the system still works, and everything you seed yourself with going forward has to be something worthy of being brought forth. The release of your ability is too great to take on anything, any person, or any thought.

Since God began a work with you, He will complete that work with you. Remember that God doesn't run out of ideas, resources, or strength. When God speaks greatness into the life of a Sarah, he speaks it into the system He created within her so that something great comes forth that will crush insecurities. This is not to say you will not have moments of frailty. You are a human being. The frail moments of Sarah do not define her entire being. You must live and decide daily from your divine definition, not consistently looking to redefine yourself. You will never grasp who you are When you are looking to redefine yourself based on past failures. You will find yourself on the run with unseeded and unsettled abilities.

The masterful acts of Sarah's will are not an accident but intentional. She is not random. She is deliberate. She releases her ability with the intended goal of making something of herself, her family, her friendships, and her goals. Don't allow yourself to be haphazard. You're too special to let your life to fly in the winds of another's emotions or float in the waters of someone else's whims. Your feelings are important. They have their role, and we will discuss them further in the book, but they are not ultimately designed to decide for you. Sarah! You are not the victim of circumstance. When you train your will, you control what is conceived in you. The usual answer to any question is yes or no, but because of the creative nature of a woman, you have a yes, a no and a "not now option." Protect your will because it determines when and what you will ultimately give to this world.

Lesson THREE: The Emotions, Expanding Your Ability

Genesis 21:2: "Sarah became pregnant and bore a son to Abraham in his old age, at the very time God had promised him."

Sarah's emotions are what allow her to expand and adapt. There is so much power in the word 'become!' God created her with an innate ability to simply become. To become is to move from one state of being to another for the sake of creating. When a woman becomes pregnant, her body automatically changes so that she can house what wants to grow there. As soon as she conceives, every part of her that will be involved in this birthing process prepares itself. This is what a woman's emotions are for. Her emotions allow her to become what she needs to survive the process. This is something men are not able to do as well. It is not part of his natural makeup. Men usually spend years in one frame of thought and action. It takes rope, bulldozers, and chainsaws to change a man's way. Whereas women naturally adapt and expand to make sure everything around her is nurtured. A woman has to grow with what is growing within. When you take on an idea, a dream, or a relationship, know that you must allow yourself to expand with what you took on as it grows and becomes more excellent. This expansion is uncomfortable at times. You must lose much of what you were to bring forth what's inside you. Your thinking will change. You won't get as much rest as usual. You'll have to find new ways to find comfort. Things you related to before don't compute like in times past. This is part of 'Becoming.' These stages can almost make you regret allowing yourself to be this remarkable, productive woman. Regret is part of the birthing process. You must know that your ability to adapt and expand is impressive and not a curse. When you watch yourself change, go with the change you see. Celebrate the various things happening in your character because you're moving from being a bondwoman to being free. Sarah's nature is to nurture. A woman who fights this side of her nature will never be delighted.

Four major factors make you tighten up when you should be adapting and readying yourself for the magnificent. These hindrances are fear, doubt, guilt, and shame. None of the four have feet that allow them to chase you down. None can get you and drag you into what you once were. Yet all four have a voice that quietly tempts you to shut down your dreams and return to the barren days. Each speaks differently, but they all can be defeated.

1. Fear tries to convince you that even if you get through the process of carrying greatness and birth it, you will not be able

to maintain it. Fear is not interested in keeping you from your now. Its' purpose is to make you afraid of the future. Fear of the future makes you feel like celebrating where you are and setting up a camp.

2. Doubt has a different agenda. Doubt says that you will not even make it through the process. Doubt doesn't make demands but instead asks questions. Doubt asks: are you sure that you're even equipped for this? Can you finish? Should you have even begun? Doubt's questions cause you to distrust yourself and become uncertain about everything. These feelings of Uncertainty make the little girl in you run for cover and forget the hope of bringing anything forth. It makes you wonder if the process is worth it at all.

3. Guilt mentions how other people may deserve this more than you. Guilt will

make you want to give away what is yours. It causes you to think outside of yourself and find a positive spin in giving up. Giving this idea away or putting it in the hands of one you feel is more capable is the key. Guilt will make you bypass your moment and have you looking later for what was in your hand just a moment ago.

4. Shame is the worst of the factors because it plays on esteem. Shame constantly searches for the string of the past that fits perfectly into the future loop and gives reason why you're not good enough to go. Shame is challenging because it doesn't stop you from seeing what's ahead. It just gives you constant reasons why you cannot reach it. Shame never allows personal forgiveness. These hindrances want you to freeze up and eventually close

down and smother the greatness growing in you.

Sarah knows that this discomfort, while it seems monumental, is only for a moment. She must allow her vision to be expanded beyond the discomfort. As you battle these hindrances, you will experience an expansion of heart, creating fresh ideas and awesome opportunities. You can grow your faith and move past fear by thinking through your life and organizing all its demands into two parts. First, decide what is important and what is not. Secondly, determine what you have the strength to do quickly! The reason you take time to determine what is essential is that you need to come to the incredible realization that everything isn't. If you allow everything to sit in the same position of importance, you will always feel inept because you're bound to miss something.

After a seminar, I was conversing with a highly gifted young woman in California. With tears in her eyes, she explained that as much as she had accomplished in life, the feeling of being scattered was too overwhelming to claim success. When I heard the word 'scattered,' I knew exactly how to instruct her. Everything she wanted was so spread out that she found herself on a chase that kept her emotionally and physically exhausted. Expanding and adapting does not mean taking on everything. It means having a better view, focus, joy, and extreme strength for the path before you.

The only way to produce a healthy family, marriage, and business is to take ownership of your life and be sure you are a happy woman. You do not want to spend your life producing painfully. Just because you have in your past doesn't mean you must continue that behavior into your future. While learning to drive, I always found myself very nervous, which didn't lend itself to a great experience. I would get frustrated and turn the car around to go home for a break.

One day, I was out driving, but he would not allow me to take my usual break. He forced me to go out again; this time, he didn't give me any instructions. He watched long enough to spot my problem and help me master it. In his dad-like voice, he paused and asked, "Chris, who controls this car?" I paused and said, "Me!" His response was, "Yes, you certainly are!" I was driving the car as if the engine was controlling me and I was just facilitating the operation. The truth is that I was the operator of the car. This big running engine couldn't do anything but sit idle without me telling it what to do. The gas pedal was waiting for me to excel. The brakes were waiting for me to press down and stop the car's motion. The steering wheel was in my hand and would turn in the direction I determined. When I grasped these concepts, my nerves were quiet, and I immediately knew how to drive. Ladies often get intimidated by the big growling engine of emotions.

If you allow the emotions to take over and go wherever they feel, ultimately leading you away from the woman you yearn to be. So I ask you, Sarah, "Who controls this car?" You cannot allow anger, hurt, fright, or frustration to control the acceleration or pause of your life's purposes. Refuse these threatening vices that come to take hold and steer you whenever they desire. So, I will tell you like my father told me! You certainly are in control! You will not allow yourself to shut down the expansion, the development, or the adaptation your soul is undertaking while making room for a tremendous future you've worked hard to receive. Your emotions are a gift from God, not a curse. Your emotions were given so you can feel and sense and grow to handle extraordinary growth. Control them; they are your slave, not your master.

I must close this chapter by explaining the peace and safety in God's promised timing. Sarah became pregnant at the time that God said she would. When God decides to make declarations over your life, everything you need for the journey is inside that declared word. That word consists of two essential components; "the how" and "the when." You shouldn't wrestle over these words or ponder them to the point of frustration. A woman's job is to receive a promise and put form to it. That is what she was made to do. Sarah, you don't have to grapple. You weren't ever made to toil. You are simply unique and graceful soil.

The "how" is the responsibility of the one who sees fit to place destiny in you. This simply means that there was a prepared place in you already. That fact alone makes you qualified to produce great things. You must be confident and know that you must expand with the thing as it grows inside your mind. When the angel approached Mary, the mother of Jesus, before he mentioned that she would be with child, he told her that she was favored among women and that the Lord was with her. These two statements are significant in the life of a Sarah. She needs to be affirmed in two ways. She must know that the jewels in her were placed there at birth. She also needs to know that certain consequential decisions she makes in life separate her from the rest. It is pertinent to know that her choice qualifies her for her chance. Surely, other women may have had the capability to birth a blessed child, but this woman had to get certain about herself and decided she was able because God made her able.

This certainty must make you expand your thoughts, understanding, and response to the upcoming transitions in life. Expansion is never an operation that can be described as beautiful. It is uncomfortable and often painful. When a woman's body prepares for a child growing in utero, her shape changes, but it's only for the beauty of what is to come. An expansion on a building is the same. Parts of that once beautiful, well-put-together building must be torn down, even destroyed, but only for the beauty of what is to come. What is being removed, shifted, or taken away during this expansion process cannot be your focus. If you allow it to be, you will cause yourself to renege on what you've pressed to become.

Lesson FOUR:
Beholding Your Ability

To behold a promise you've carried forever finally has the incredible power of making you forget the pain. It wouldn't be fair to end our conversation discussing pain because it has a purpose, which is more important. When you've committed to changing your mind and believing that you can be productive, there's no need to revisit the trap that you were in. After you've battled your stubborn will, decide what you will accomplish instead of fantasizing about what you could have. At this point, there is no turning around. It's all about getting this dream, this desire, this thing that was once only a hope into your reality. The constant mulling over of pain and what you could have done better is what keeps women from going forward. These are the moments when you must disregard the journal of regrets and disappointments and know that every up and down was grandly weaved to get something powerful out of you. At the end of almost every seminar I teach, I remind the audience that they are only blessed to be a blessing. You are gifted to give gifts away. This is the virtue of becoming great, even if the journey to greatness seemed disastrous.

The most challenging area for a woman is embarrassment. For her to be made ashamed is damning to her excitement about greatness coming from her. This shame can be so harsh that it causes a highly uncomfortable self-consciousness. Two things happen when you allow your past to be a tie that binds instead of a testament of endurance.

1. Vacant esteem renders a woman voiceless and, in a position, where she is defined only by other people's

opinions. Vacant esteem makes her believe she is unworthy of birthing anything of her own.

2. Low esteem allows her to believe in herself, but the level of that esteem is so low that she allows herself to ponder her abilities and inabilities until the time of her strength passes her by.

Either of these vices will hinder you from being the blessing you're blessed to be. This is why you cannot entertain the belief that each negative occurrence defines who you are and what you can offer the world. Nor can you believe that every favorable occasion of your life defines you, but the concoction of it all, under heaven's watchful hand, has brewed such a wonderful gift within you. Now, it is your time to bypass the pain and produce a significant blessing.

In this conversation, I wanted to convey that a woman is blessed just because she is born. She is born with a systematic way to be blessed. She can receive, form, grow, and bring forth anything. This is incredibly powerful. This power you all possess caused me to write this long letter to you fearfully. I could not let you live another day without telling you that you are too admirable to allow anything in and too wonderful to possess the greatness you are forced to live without.

A Daughter's Response, Morgan Winters:

I never realized the importance of my mother until my mid-teens. I heard how valuable moms were, but as I matured, I could see it with my eyes. I was able to understand what a valued woman looked like. As my dad wrote, moms continue to "birth" you and show you the way. I think mothers do that because they know what they want for their children and feel responsible for helping them. I learned what compassion was in this book and how a woman uses it to guide herself and her family. My mother helps me with a lot of things and guided me through ups and downs. People may think mothers' advice is false and don't understand how we feel, but they do. It took a while to understand it, and at the time, I still battled to go to her, but she was strong and available. I learned that we are people who can do anything.

Girls have to know what and what not to allow into their lives. When you are going through life, people will try to take control of you, but you can't let people push and pull you. Take control of your life; don't let others do it for you. Women are so valuable that men will try to take control and manipulate them. Don't let a man abuse you mentally, physically, and emotionally. Who is the male figure in your life that is good to you? Mine is my father; he is a good man who cares for me. He respects me and is a great dad.

1. *What does a good man mean to you? (You need an example. It doesn't have to be your dad but another adult family member who will teach and guard you, too!) What do they do that helps you better define a good man?*

When going through life, your mind will try to control you, but you can't let that happen. There was a time when I let that happen, and I didn't listen to my heart and others, leading to dire consequences. You are in control of what your mind is open to.

2. *Was there a time when you let your mind become your master?*

Going through life, you must learn that you can't do everything alone; you must work with others. When you want something, you have to change your mind, which will heal you so you can get going and enjoy it! You can't have a closed mind when going through things because if you do, you won't get where you desire. There is more than one way of thinking. You have a right to think, and you should.

3. *When in life did you have a closed mind?*

Don't let people overwork you because if you do, it will leave you exhausted with no room for yourself. You have to listen to God throughout life because he will help you every step of the way. People think that God might not be there, but he is, and you just have to open your ears and eyes.

Was there a time you let opportunities pass by because your mind wasn't releasing anything helpful?

Life isn't easy, but if you listen to God and expand your mind, you'll be alright. There will be times when you will have to fight, but you got this! You must find your identity and all the great things God made you to accomplish. Many girls think their past mistakes define them, but it doesn't. Your past is not yours, and you must understand to make your life a little easier. Many people know versions of you that don't exist anymore, and that's ok. When it comes to friends, pick them wisely. People can be very fake and play you, so having two real friends is okay because that's better than having ten fake ones.

When discussing your success, notice how your friends act because that can show their true colors. Notice how backstabbing doesn't come from your enemies but from people, you call your best friends. Life will cause you to have so much wisdom, and that's a good thing. Share that wisdom with people because somebody might need it.

When you feel like you can't do anything, tell yourself you will. You need yourself more than anything! It may not be easy to change, but it's worth it. Don't let your feelings control you; fix them. Your daily decision is to work hard for what you want or sit back and do nothing. Many girls are in toxic situations, and that's not okay. Remember to stay strong and be cautious with who you bring into your life and what things you get. Be strong like a lion. Everyone has a gift in life; you just have to find yours.

God created you and began working with you; he will complete that work, so trust him.

Control yourself in life because if you don't, that will lead to many destructive paths, which is unhealthy. I got into many fights in school, and I was the only one that got in trouble no matter whether I hit first because I started the altercation that led to the fight. I never understood that until I got suspended, and none of my "friends" stuck by my side. They all left. I had to learn the hard way to control my emotions and to be cautious with people.

Was there a time when you didn't control yourself, and what was the outcome of it?

You will go through a lot to mature and become better; you will lose a lot of things, but it will be worth it. It will be worth it because you will be happier. Don't let negative emotions control you; fight them with your love for yourself and your future. Guilt can control and trick you, but you must be strong and keep pushing. Shame can affect your self-esteem; the most essential thing you must remember is to love yourself. No one can bother you and hurt you when you love yourself because you know yourself enough not to be hindered by it.

Everything in life is not necessary or worth your energy. Believing that it is only weakens you. Let God take control of your life; he won't fail you. Expand on things you love and explore because life is better with adventure in it.

- A. Commit to changing your mind, and you will be very productive.
- B. Learn not to be stubborn. You will see so many things differently when you have an open mind.
- C. You will go through disappointment, but keep your mind strong.

D. Remember to stay strong and know God will be by your side through it all.

Think about a time when you explored an adventure, and was it fun? Did you have an open mind at that moment? You are loved, fabulous, fearless, beautiful, and more. Always remember that. Being a woman is impressive. You will grow a lot, be blessed, and can do anything.

Your friend
Morgan

Lesson Five: How To Know Identify Who To Say I Do To?

Whenever I have the privilege to teach women, I get asked a brilliant question in a few different variations.

1. "Christian, any guy can ask for my hand in marriage, but how do I know whether he's the right guy?"
2. "If a man chooses me, don't you have a right to choose, too?"
3. "Christian, what should I be looking for?"

I think the answer lies inside the first wedding. Yes! There was a wedding in that great book of beginnings. Let's take a look at two scriptures.

"Then the Lord God said, "It is not good for the man to be alone. I will make a helper who is just right for him."

Genesis 2:18 NLT

So the Lord God caused the man to fall into a deep sleep. While the man slept, the Lord God took out one of the man's ribs and closed up the opening. Then the Lord God made a woman from the rib, and he brought her to the man. "At last!" the man exclaimed. "This one is bone from my bone and flesh from my flesh! She will be called 'woman' because she was taken from 'man.'

Genesis 2:21-23 NLT

First, we have God saying that it is not good for man to be alone. Some scholars have interpreted this to mean that 'it is no longer good for man to be alone.' I understand this interpolation because it must have been a time

The Soul of Sarah

that it was, or God would have given Adam his Eve immediately. He didn't because men must understand who they are, where they are going, and what they need before properly perceiving their mate. After he has ahold of those three virtues, it is no longer good for him to be alone. Why? All of that is too much for him to handle alone. He needed the mixture which I call "intimate wisdom." A woman who ministers to a side of him that God himself could not. A godly woman is wisdom embodied. This is why wisdom is referred to as "she" in the scriptures. Though God was there with Adam, he had a need that left him alone. That's the power of a wife. That's something you must become before you say I do. Ladies! Not only should you withhold your vagina, you should also withhold your deposit of wisdom. You have no obligation to help build a thing you will never have keys to.

A readied man should have a readied woman. God took something from man: a rib! Which is complete sturdiness. As I wrote earlier, He was missing the ability to create, and now he was unsteady. So, he had to lay down. God puts him in a deep sleep because what would a man do if he had to admit what he doesn't have while wide awake? But what woman wants to walk around awake and admit what she doesn't know? I would love to put an emoji there, but that's not professional. This man needs a woman. The woman needs the man no matter what poison society is pushing about the necessity of sharing your world. God makes a woman out of the very thing he took from man. Ladies, that means the first thing you need to become in the hands of God is sturdy, aka being able to uphold. Uphold what, Christian? The vision that your man has allowed God to put in his heart.

So how do you know who to give all this goodness to? *Now you see how much you have to offer aside from your body?!*

The First Wedding

God took that rib, which means it was taken surgically. It was not ripped out. She was delicately removed by God's hand. A surgeon cleans what he removes so that he can see it. I believe that represents the washing of the word of God. How will you be "wisdom" to him if you don't understand the word of God and when to apply it to your husband? Again, you are still in the grip of God's hand. This sturdy rib was walked through life's ups and downs, but every time, she was in the grip of God. As you read these words, I'm sure flashes of memories dance through your mind of times when you found yourself brave and broken but in the grip of God.

You have to remember that loving grip when you are dating a man. It is your guide to identifying your husband. He won't always have the perfect grip, just like you won't always sound like ideal wisdom, but you know when it's sincere when God stood at the top of the wedding aisle holding this rib. The Holy Spirit stood at the aisle's other end, waiting to officiate. As your father walks you closer and closer to this prepared man, you feel the father's grip loosening, and with fear, you wonder why. You tremble until you hear the officiant ask who gives this woman? God, with authority, replies I do! The man that's been courting you reaches to take you from your father, and the exact grip you've felt Throughout your walk with God and through your dating process it does not change! That is your husband.

That's why you must walk with God throughout your life so you know what a proper grip feels like. Let him lead you to a passport office. Let him inspire you to see the great big world. Allow Him to take you on a scroll through your desires and dig through to discover which one is your purpose. You and your husband should take the same strolls and feel the exact grip.

Don't abandon all you've become by submitting it to the wrong man, dear daughter; he should walk with you on the level you've been on and, at some point, take you higher.

Love Dad

Made in the USA
Columbia, SC
23 April 2025